THE
BETTER HALF

BY
RANDY GLASBERGEN

CCC PUBLICATIONS

Published by

CCC Publications
1111 Rancho Conejo Blvd.
Suites 411 & 412
Newbury Park, CA 91320

Under arrangement with King Features Syndicate, Inc.

Manufactured in the United States of America

Cover & interior art by Randy Glasbergen

Cover/Interior production by Oasis Graphics

ISBN: 1-57644-036-2

If your local U.S. bookstore is out of stock, copies of this book may be obtained by mailing check or money order for
$5.95 per book (plus $2.75 to cover postage and handling) to: CCC Publications, 1111 Rancho Conejo Blvd.,
Suites 411 & 412, Newbury Park, CA 91320

Pre-publication Edition - 9/96

Introduction

Despite rumors to the contrary, cartoonist Randy Glasbergen has **NOT** been peeking in your windows!

If these cartoons remind you of your husband, wife, parents or neighbors it's not because Randy Glasbergen has been spying on people. But he has been observing human behavior and turning it into hilarious cartoons for more than 20 years! His gentle jabs have made him one of America's favorite cartoonists, appearing in hundreds of newspapers and magazines around the world.

In this first collection of his cartoons from "**The Better Half**," Glasbergen takes a twisted and insightful look at modern marriage and the ongoing battle of the sexes.

If the cartoons in this book sound like they were written about you or someone you know, it's only a coincidence. But from now on, you better keep your shades pulled down . . . just in case!

"We want to go someplace where dull people with no money and no energy can have the time of their lives."

"I wasn't crying because the movie was so sad. I was crying because we couldn't watch the program I wanted."

"How are we supposed to grow old together
if you get more immature every year?"

"I got too close to your dirty sneakers.
Then suddenly I was in this tunnel with a very bright light..."

"It's like dating – it's hard for men to commit to one channel
if there might be better stuff on other channels!"

"If I have a guardian angel who watches over me,
how come she let me get married?!?"

"Both men and women like this one. There's a wild car chase and a lot of explosions, then they all talk about it."

S

"You and I make a good team,
but I wish we'd score more often!"

"My wife says I should be more sensitive.
So when she asks me to take out the trash, I cry."

"I accept you for what you are.
What you are is someone who is going to change or else!"

"I'm no mechanic, but I'm pretty sure
that's not how you change the oil."

"You shouldn't let society tell you what to eat,
how to dress or what to think – that's MY job!"

"So a man at work bought me a wedding dress –
everybody flirts!"

Fitness Equipment

"What do you suggest for a husband who thinks the handle on his recliner is an exercise machine?"

"My male encounter group gets together every week to share our feelings. Mostly we feel like playing poker."

"How can you say I'm not romantic?
Just yesterday I faxed you a picture of some flowers!"

"Whenever my life seems dull, I watch golf on TV and suddenly everything else looks a lot more exciting!"

"Night after night, I see commercials for every imaginable female ailment – and you wonder why I'm not more romantic?!?"

"You have bad handwriting.
'Tofu and bean sprouts' looks like 'beer and pizza'!"

"I can kiss you longer if I know
I'm not missing anything good on TV!"

"Normally I don't notice such things,
but did you change your mascara?"

"Sure, I trust you . . . I trust you to behave like a man!
That's why I don't trust you!"

"You know what's the problem with marriage?
There's no room for advancement!"

"When it comes to romance, my Stanley is an animal . . .
the kind you find on the side of the highway!"

"I only overeat when I'm under stress.
And dieting is *very* stressful!"

"You know, at $75 a session it's in her best interest to keep us unhappy for as long as possible!"

"Starting today I'm going to be a lot nicer to everyone.
Hey, bozo, I'm talking to you!"

"Her kisses are sweeter than wine
. . . but I'm a beer man!"

"If you tape telemarketers and play it back to them, they buy stuff from themselves!"

"I've been working too hard lately and I really need a vacation. Please fax the butter."

"Bess is getting married, so I'm taking up a collection to send her away until she comes to her senses."

"I'm making a grocery list. Do we still care which foods will kill us or have we finally accepted the fact that we won't live forever?"

"The next time you borrow my razor to shave your legs,
I'm going to borrow your toothbrush to clean my ears!"

"When I do the laundry in the dark, everything looks sort of gray.
That way I don't have to sort the colors!"

"I've never had an out-of-body experience,
but I've had several out-of-money experiences."

"My heart burns so bright for you, if it wasn't insulated by all this fat, we'd both go up in flames!"

"I'm sure these marriage-improvement tapes will help. When we're listening to them, we don't have to listen to each other!"

"It's 100 degrees, the air conditioner doesn't work . . . so how is it possible that you still come to bed with ice-cold feet?"

"I try not to think too much.
With this bald head, an oversized brain would look creepy."

"You're not as much fun as you used to be –
and you used to be really dull!"

"I plan to retire from marriage at age 65.
I thought you knew that!"

"We are home, but we're busy arguing over who's going to answer the phone. Please leave a message."

"Stanley says women talk too much about their feelings. How do you feel when men say stuff like that?"

"It's a donor card. When I die, I'm going to leave all my charm and personality to a dull person!"

"I'm really tired tonight. Do you mind if
I kiss good night with only one lip?"

"You've made your point, Stanley.
I apologize for calling you boring and predictable!"

"Once I sipped champagne from Harriet's slipper –
nearly choked to death on an old bunion pad!"

"Are you not speaking to me because you're angry or have my stunning good looks left you speechless?"

"When a cat purrs, it means she loves you and enjoys being close to you. It's the same thing when I snore."

"Our accountant says our long-range financial plan should include anything we find under the sofa cushions."

"I got in touch with my feelings once. They told me to leave them alone and mind my own business!"

"Stanley's manners are improving. He still clips his toenails during dinner, but now he aims them away from my food."

"Most women get bored looking at the same face every morning. But making new faces won't help!"

"This CD-ROM is just for husbands. It contains 5,000 apologies and excuses for every occasion."

"Before you order the exercise machine, find out if it's light enough for me to carry outside for our next garage sale."

"I know you hate getting older, but telling people you're 'thirtyeighteen' just confuses them."

"I have a wonderful personality . . .
but I'm saving it for a special occasion."

"My wife says I'm lazy. I'd like to tell her how wrong she is, but it's just too much bother."

"Just when I thought Stanley's eating habits couldn't get any worse, he started drinking gravy as a beverage."

"I may need glasses.
I'm finding it harder to see past your faults!"

"I don't like to be called a 'wife.'
I prefer the term 'romantically challenged'!"

"It's a list of 100 things you can talk
to me about besides your job!"

"I don't expect you to be cheerful 24 hours a day.
Just act excited like a poodle whenever I enter the room!"

"I understand about males being more aggressive, Stanley, but footsie shouldn't be played for points!"

"That's it? I've had longer back massages
during a game of tag!"

"It says: 'I am a TV addict.
In case of emergency tape my programs.'"

"I'm *almost* a vegetarian. I eat grass and grain after it's been turned into a cow or pig."

"Your wife wants you to bring home a loaf of bread,
a gallon of milk and a halfway decent attitude."

"Help! I think my husband is in a coma!
It's been over three minutes since he changed channels!"

"I'm not in the mood for soup, but I need something to dump on your head if you keep flirting with the waitress."

"When I die, I want my ashes scattered wherever they'll most annoy your next wife."

"The TV isn't working, so Stanley is outside watching the bug zapper."

"I like being married to a dull person. By comparison, it makes me seem a lot more interesting than I really am!"

"You installed a speed bump in front of the refrigerator?"

"Let's do something romantic tonight. Let's go to bed at 6:30, before we get on each other's nerves."

"You're not fooling me, Stanley.
That's a kielbasa!"

"Stanley likes to keep score. He won't give me a compliment unless I sign for it and give him a receipt!"

"That's how I keep in shape, Stanley . . .
I make **you** bigger so **I** look smaller!"

"Hi, this is your wife. To say I look nice today, press *one*. To say you miss me, press *two*. To say you can't live without me, press *three*..."

"Make sure my husband receives the *exact* same number of fries as I do . . . or things could get ugly!"

"I like country music, but my wife likes classical. To compromise, do you have an opera about cheating truck drivers?"

"What do you mean we don't spend enough time together?
I sleep with you for eight hours every night!"

"I don't want you to smell irresistible.
I want you to smell married."

"Candlelight dinners aren't very romantic.
Every time I lean over to kiss you, my nose hair catches on fire."

"This is only my first marriage. For a man with no prior husband experience, I'm not doing so badly!"

"Remember the song they were playing the very first time we kissed? It's a hemorrhoid jingle now."

"I guess things are different today. It used to be impolite for the groom to bring a date to his wedding."

"What do you think? Are we really happy together . . .
or are we just too tired to fight?"

"Your kisses were supposed to knock my socks off, but they knocked by hair off instead."

"If you really loved me, you'd get me an aspirin . . .
especially since you're the one who gave me the headache!"

"I don't want to change you, Stanley.
But it would be nice if you had a fine-tuning knob!"

"I want a card to tell my wife I love her more than anything else in the world. Got any cheaper ones?"

"Let's scream at each other, just so the neighbors won't think we're dull."

"If I could live my life over, yes, I'd marry you again.
The food at our wedding reception was fantastic!"

"I think we should renew our vows. There's 50 pounds of you that wasn't at our first wedding."

"My psychic gave me a discount
because you're so predictable."

"Our guests will be here in 10 minutes!
Please try to be in a good mood!"

"Please tell me what's troubling you. I'd like to help you if I can. But be quick because the commercial is almost over."

"It's cheaper than a real baby and we get a
new tape every month until he turns 21!"

"If we're both gonna share the housework equally, you've got to get a lot lazier!"

"I don't need a psychic to predict your future,
I just need a TV guide."

"I'd like romantic movies better if every time
somebody kissed something blew up."

"He keeps two pictures in his wallet.
One of me and one of the TV."

"Thank you for calling the Women's Forum. If your man is a jerk, ss 1. If your man is a loser, press 2. If your man is a geek, press 3..."

"We could move back in with my parents,
but they just moved back in with *their* parents!"

"We used to gaze into each other's eyes for hours. Maybe there weren't any good TV shows that year."

"You didn't look like that on our first date.
I could sue you for false advertising!"

"*Finally*, something we can *both* enjoy!
A ballet where the dancers tackle each other!"

"It's not really a belly. It's the warehouse where I keep all my love for you!"

"Breakfast is the most important meal of the day –
that's when I decide whether to put up with you for another day!"

"I worked out a schedule: you hog the covers from 11:00-1:00, then I hog them from 1:00-3:00, then you...."

"If I treat you nice, you'll expect the whole world to treat you nice! I'd just be setting you up for disappointment!"

"Your horoscope says you're going to enjoy a romantic month!
Are you seeing someone else?"

"Throw your gum away when you kiss me –
don't just stick it behind my ear!"

"My husband and I are hopelessly incompatible.
He's a man and I'm a woman!"

TITLES BY CCC PUBLICATIONS

Retail $4.99
"?" book
POSITIVELY PREGNANT
CAN SEX IMPROVE YOUR GOLF?
THE COMPLETE BOOGER BOOK
FLYING FUNNIES
MARITAL BLISS & OXYMORONS
THE VERY VERY SEXY ADULT DOT-TO-DOT BOOK
THE DEFINITIVE FART BOOK
THE COMPLETE WIMP'S GUIDE TO SEX
THE CAT OWNER'S SHAPE UP MANUAL
RETIRED: LET THE GAMES BEGIN
THE OFFICE FROM HELL
FOOD & SEX
FITNESS FANATICS
YOUNGER MEN ARE BETTER THAN RETIN-A
BUT OSSIFER, IT'S NOT MY FAULT

Retail $4.95
YOU KNOW YOU'RE AN OLD FART WHEN...
1001 WAYS TO PROCRASTINATE
HORMONES FROM HELL II
SHARING THE ROAD WITH IDIOTS
GREATEST ANSWERING MACHINE MESSAGES
WHAT DO WE DO NOW?? (A Guide For New Parents)
HOW TO TALK YOU WAY OUT OF
  A TRAFFIC TICKET
THE BOTTOM HALF (Spot Incompetent Professionals)
LIFE'S MOST EMBARRASSING MOMENTS
HOW TO ENTERTAIN PEOPLE YOU HATE
YOUR GUIDE TO CORPORATE SURVIVAL
GUIDE TO EVERYDAY IRRITATIONS
GIFTING RIGHT

Retail $5.95
THE ART OF MOONING
THE BOOK OF WHITE TRASH
CORPORATE LIES
THE BETTER HALF
THE BASTARD'S GUIDE TO GOLF
PMS CRAZED: TOUCH ME AND I'LL KILL YOU!
WHY MEN ARE CLUELESS
CRINKLED 'N' WRINKLED
SMART COMEBACKS FOR STUPID QUESTIONS
YIKES! IT'S ANOTHER BIRTHDAY
SEX IS A GAME
SEX AND YOUR STARS
SIGNS YOUR SEX LIFE IS DEAD
40 AND HOLDING YOUR OWN
50 AND HOLDING YOUR OWN
MALE BASHING: WOMEN'S FAVORITE PASTIME
THINGS YOU CAN DO WITH A USELESS MAN
MORE THINGS YOU CAN DO WITH A
  USELESS MAN
THE WORLD'S GREATEST PUT-DOWN LINES
LITTLE INSTRUCTION BOOK OF THE
  RICH & FAMOUS
WELCOME TO YOUR MIDLIFE CRISIS
GETTING EVEN WITH THE ANSWERING MACHINE
ARE YOU A SPORTS NUT?
MEN ARE PIGS / WOMEN ARE BITCHES
ARE WE DYSFUNCTIONAL YET?
TECHNOLOGY BYTES!
50 WAYS TO HUSTLE YOUR FRIENDS ($5.99)
HORMONES FROM HELL
HUSBANDS FROM HELL
KILLER BRAS & Other Hazards Of The 50's
IT'S BETTER TO BE OVER THE HILL
  THAN UNDER IT

HOW TO REALLY PARTY!!!
WORK SUCKS!
THE PEOPLE WATCHER'S FIELD GUIDE
THE UNOFFICIAL WOMEN'S DIVORCE GUIDE
THE ABSOLUTE LAST CHANCE DIET BOOK
FOR MEN ONLY (How To Survive Marriage)
THE UGLY TRUTH ABOUT MEN
NEVER A DULL CARD
LOVE DAT CAT ($6.95)
RED HOT MONOGAMY ($6.95)
HOW TO SURVIVE A JEWISH MOTHER ($6.95)
WHY MEN DON'T HAVE A CLUE ($7.99)
LADIES, START YOUR ENGINES! ($7.99)

Retail $3.95
NO HANG-UPS
NO HANG-UPS II
NO HANG-UPS III
HOW TO SUCCEED IN SINGLES BARS
HOW TO GET EVEN WITH YOUR EXES
OUTRAGEOUS BUMPER-SNICKERS ($2.95)

NO HANG-UPS – CASSETTES Retail $4.98
Vol. I: GENERAL MESSAGES (Female)
Vol. I: GENERAL MESSAGES (Male)
Vol. II: BUSINESS MESSAGES (Female)
Vol. II: BUSINESS MESSAGES (Male)
Vol. III: 'R' RATED MESSAGES (Female)
Vol. III: 'R' RATED MESSAGES (Male)
Vol. IV: SOUND EFFECTS ONLY
Vol. V: CELEBRI-TEASE